# My Bucket List

## Living the Dream

By Barbara Paulding

PETER PAUPER PRESS, INC.
WHITE PLAINS, NEW YORK

PETER PAUPER PRESS
*Fine Books and Gifts Since 1928*

## Our Company

In 1928, at the age of twenty-two, Peter Beilenson began printing books on a small press in the basement of his parents' home in Larchmont, New York. Peter—and later, his wife, Edna—sought to create fine books that sold at "prices even a pauper could afford."

Today, still family owned and operated, Peter Pauper Press continues to honor our founders' legacy—and our customers' expectations—of beauty, quality, and value.

Designed by Heather Zschock

Images used under license from Shutterstock.com


Peter Pauper Press, Inc.
202 Mamaroneck Avenue
White Plains, NY 10601

ISBN 978-1-4413-3106-9
Printed in China
14 13 12 11 10 9 8

Visit us at www.peterpauper.com

# CONTENTS



*I haven't been everywhere, but it's on my list.*

SUSAN SONTAG

# INTRODUCTION

*The bad news is time flies.*
*The good news is you're the pilot.*

MICHAEL ALTSHULER

Ever feel like the years roll by while your dreams and intentions get shunted aside with the busy day-to-day? Here's the secret to making them happen: *Write them down*! This glorious wish list—your **Bucket List**—will help you articulate, organize, remember, prioritize, plan for, and accomplish your dreams both large and small.

*Most* items on a **Bucket List** are:

- **Places to go** and **adventures to have**, so *most* of this journal is dedicated to them.

Also important are other categories that have their own sections in the back, along with suggestions and checklists:

- **Books to read**
- **Movies and shows to see**
- **Foodie experiences to relish**
- **Good works to do**
- **Things to learn and achieve**

Concise wish lists, with priority ratings and dates completed, help keep intentions on your radar. Suggestions throughout provide inspiring examples worthy of a Bucket List. In the first, main section, pages of fill-in prompts guide you to write down the before and after planning and details of 65 adventures.

*Let the games begin!*

# PLACES TO GO & ADVENTURES TO HAVE

*We live in a wonderful world that is full of beauty, charm, and adventure.There is no end to the adventures that we can have if only we seek them with our eyes open.*

JAWAHARLAL NEHRU

The world is brimming with places to go and adventures to have. Perhaps you dream of wandering down the Champs-Élysées in the City of Light, tölting on an Icelandic horse beneath the Northern Lights, skiing the steeps in the Chilean Andes, experiencing Burning Man in Nevada, snorkeling in the Great Barrier Reef, cruising around the Seychelles, ecotouring in the Amazon, hot air ballooning over Sedona, or anything you can imagine in the realm of possibility. Satisfy that wanderlust! As Ray Bradbury wrote, "Stuff your eyes with wonder."

# PLACES TO GO & ADVENTURES TO HAVE

## Wish List

| PLACES TO GO & ADVENTURES TO HAVE | PRIORITY RATING (1-10) | I DID IT! (DATE) |
|---|---|---|
| | | |
| | | |
| | | |
| | | |
| | | |
| | | |
| | | |
| | | |
| | | |
| | | |
| | | |
| | | |
| | | |
| | | |
| | | |

| PLACES TO GO & ADVENTURES TO HAVE | PRIORITY RATING (1-10) | I DID IT! (DATE) |
|---|---|---|
| | | |
| | | |
| | | |
| | | |
| | | |
| | | |
| | | |
| | | |
| | | |
| | | |
| | | |
| | | |
| | | |
| | | |
| | | |
| | | |
| | | |
| | | |
| | | |

| PLACES TO GO & ADVENTURES TO HAVE | PRIORITY RATING (1-10) | I DID IT! (DATE) |
|---|---|---|
| | | |
| | | |
| | | |
| | | |
| | | |
| | | |
| | | |
| | | |
| | | |
| | | |
| | | |
| | | |
| | | |
| | | |
| | | |
| | | |
| | | |
| | | |
| | | |

| PLACES TO GO & ADVENTURES TO HAVE | PRIORITY RATING (1-10) | I DID IT! (DATE) |
|---|---|---|
| | | |
| | | |
| | | |
| | | |
| | | |
| | | |
| | | |
| | | |
| | | |
| | | |
| | | |
| | | |
| | | |
| | | |
| | | |
| | | |
| | | |
| | | |
| | | |

# PLACE OR ADVENTURE:

**Target date:**

**Cost:**

**How to make it happen:**

**Planning details** (who with, where to stay, how to get there, what to bring):

Date completed:

Highlights:

People who made it special:

What surprised me most:

Did it live up to my expectations?

1 2 3 4 5 6 7 8 9 10

## PLACE OR ADVENTURE:

**Target date:**

**Cost:**

**How to make it happen:**

**Planning details** (who with, where to stay, how to get there, what to bring):

Date completed:

Highlights:

People who made it special:

What surprised me most:

Did it live up to my expectations?

1 2 3 4 5 6 7 8 9 10

# PLACE OR ADVENTURE:

Target date:

Cost:

How to make it happen:

**Planning details** (who with, where to stay, how to get there, what to bring):

Date completed:

Highlights:

People who made it special:

What surprised me most:

Did it live up to my expectations?

1 2 3 4 5 6 7 8 9 10

# PLACE OR ADVENTURE:

**Target date:**

**Cost:**

**How to make it happen:**

**Planning details** (who with, where to stay, how to get there, what to bring):

Date completed:

Highlights:

People who made it special:

What surprised me most:

Did it live up to my expectations?

1 2 3 4 5 6 7 8 9 10

## PLACE OR ADVENTURE:

Target date:

Cost:

How to make it happen:

**Planning details** (who with, where to stay, how to get there, what to bring):

Date completed: ..........

Highlights: ..........

People who made it special: ..........

What surprised me most: ..........

Did it live up to my expectations?

1 2 3 4 5 6 7 8 9 10

# PLACE OR ADVENTURE:

..............................................................................................................

..............................................................................................................

..............................................................................................................

..............................................................................................................

**Target date:** ..............................................................................................

**Cost:** .......................................................................................................

**How to make it happen:** ..............................................................................

..............................................................................................................

..............................................................................................................

..............................................................................................................

..............................................................................................................

**Planning details** (who with, where to stay, how to get there, what to bring):

..............................................................................................................

..............................................................................................................

..............................................................................................................

..............................................................................................................

..............................................................................................................

..............................................................................................................

..............................................................................................................

..............................................................................................................

Date completed:

Highlights:

People who made it special:

What surprised me most:

Did it live up to my expectations?

1 2 3 4 5 6 7 8 9 10

## PLACE OR ADVENTURE:

**Target date:**

**Cost:**

**How to make it happen:**

**Planning details** (who with, where to stay, how to get there, what to bring):

Date completed:

Highlights:

People who made it special:

What surprised me most:

Did it live up to my expectations?

1 2 3 4 5 6 7 8 9 10

## PLACE OR ADVENTURE:

Target date:

Cost:

How to make it happen:

**Planning details** (who with, where to stay, how to get there, what to bring):

Date completed:

Highlights:

People who made it special:

What surprised me most:

Did it live up to my expectations?

1 2 3 4 5 6 7 8 9 10

## PLACE OR ADVENTURE:

**Target date:**

**Cost:**

**How to make it happen:**

**Planning details** (who with, where to stay, how to get there, what to bring):

Date completed:

Highlights:

People who made it special:

What surprised me most:

Did it live up to my expectations?

1 2 3 4 5 6 7 8 9 10

## PLACE OR ADVENTURE:

Target date:

Cost:

How to make it happen:

**Planning details** (who with, where to stay, how to get there, what to bring):

Date completed:

Highlights:

People who made it special:

What surprised me most:

Did it live up to my expectations?

1 2 3 4 5 6 7 8 9 10

## PLACE OR ADVENTURE:

Target date:

Cost:

How to make it happen:

**Planning details** (who with, where to stay, how to get there, what to bring):

Date completed:

Highlights:

People who made it special:

What surprised me most:

Did it live up to my expectations?

1 2 3 4 5 6 7 8 9 10

## PLACE OR ADVENTURE:

**Target date:**

**Cost:**

**How to make it happen:**

**Planning details** (who with, where to stay, how to get there, what to bring):

Date completed:

Highlights:

People who made it special:

What surprised me most:

Did it live up to my expectations?

1 2 3 4 5 6 7 8 9 10

## PLACE OR ADVENTURE:

**Target date:**

**Cost:**

**How to make it happen:**

**Planning details** (who with, where to stay, how to get there, what to bring):

Date completed:

Highlights:

People who made it special:

What surprised me most:

Did it live up to my expectations?

1 2 3 4 5 6 7 8 9 10

## PLACE OR ADVENTURE:

**Target date:**

**Cost:**

**How to make it happen:**

**Planning details** (who with, where to stay, how to get there, what to bring):

Date completed: ..........

Highlights: ..........

People who made it special: ..........

What surprised me most: ..........

Did it live up to my expectations?

1 2 3 4 5 6 7 8 9 10

## PLACE OR ADVENTURE:

**Target date:**

**Cost:**

**How to make it happen:**

**Planning details** (who with, where to stay, how to get there, what to bring):

Date completed:

Highlights:

People who made it special:

What surprised me most:

Did it live up to my expectations?

1 2 3 4 5 6 7 8 9 10

## PLACE OR ADVENTURE:

**Target date:**

**Cost:**

**How to make it happen:**

**Planning details** (who with, where to stay, how to get there, what to bring):

Date completed:

Highlights:

People who made it special:

What surprised me most:

Did it live up to my expectations?

1 2 3 4 5 6 7 8 9 10

## PLACE OR ADVENTURE:

**Target date:**

**Cost:**

**How to make it happen:**

**Planning details** (who with, where to stay, how to get there, what to bring):

Date completed:

Highlights:

People who made it special:

What surprised me most:

Did it live up to my expectations?

1 2 3 4 5 6 7 8 9 10

# PLACE OR ADVENTURE:

**Target date:**

**Cost:**

**How to make it happen:**

**Planning details** (who with, where to stay, how to get there, what to bring):

Date completed:

Highlights:

People who made it special:

What surprised me most:

Did it live up to my expectations?

1 2 3 4 5 6 7 8 9 10

## PLACE OR ADVENTURE:

**Target date:**

**Cost:**

**How to make it happen:**

**Planning details** (who with, where to stay, how to get there, what to bring):

Date completed:

Highlights:

People who made it special:

What surprised me most:

Did it live up to my expectations?

1 2 3 4 5 6 7 8 9 10

## PLACE OR ADVENTURE:

..........

..........

..........

..........

**Target date:** ..........

**Cost:** ..........

**How to make it happen:** ..........

..........

..........

..........

..........

**Planning details** (who with, where to stay, how to get there, what to bring):

..........

..........

..........

..........

..........

..........

..........

..........

Date completed:

Highlights:

People who made it special:

What surprised me most:

Did it live up to my expectations?

1 2 3 4 5 6 7 8 9 10

## PLACE OR ADVENTURE:

........................................

........................................

........................................

........................................

**Target date:** ........................................

**Cost:** ........................................

**How to make it happen:** ........................................

........................................

........................................

........................................

........................................

**Planning details** (who with, where to stay, how to get there, what to bring):

........................................

........................................

........................................

........................................

........................................

........................................

........................................

........................................

Date completed:

Highlights:

People who made it special:

What surprised me most:

Did it live up to my expectations?

1 2 3 4 5 6 7 8 9 10

## PLACE OR ADVENTURE:

Target date:

Cost:

How to make it happen:

**Planning details** (who with, where to stay, how to get there, what to bring):

Date completed:

Highlights:

People who made it special:

What surprised me most:

Did it live up to my expectations?

1 2 3 4 5 6 7 8 9 10

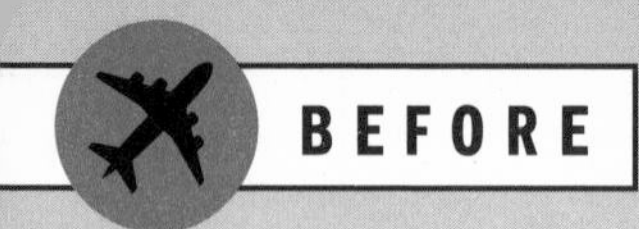


## PLACE OR ADVENTURE:

**Target date:**

**Cost:**

**How to make it happen:**

**Planning details** (who with, where to stay, how to get there, what to bring):

Date completed:

Highlights:

People who made it special:

What surprised me most:

Did it live up to my expectations?

1 2 3 4 5 6 7 8 9 10

# PLACE OR ADVENTURE:

**Target date:**

**Cost:**

**How to make it happen:**

**Planning details** (who with, where to stay, how to get there, what to bring):

Date completed: ..............................

Highlights: ..............................

People who made it special: ..............................

What surprised me most: ..............................

Did it live up to my expectations?

1 2 3 4 5 6 7 8 9 10

# PLACE OR ADVENTURE:

**Target date:**

**Cost:**

**How to make it happen:**

**Planning details** (who with, where to stay, how to get there, what to bring):

Date completed: ..........

Highlights: ..........

People who made it special: ..........

What surprised me most: ..........

Did it live up to my expectations?

1 2 3 4 5 6 7 8 9 10

## PLACE OR ADVENTURE:

**Target date:**

**Cost:**

**How to make it happen:**

**Planning details** (who with, where to stay, how to get there, what to bring):

Date completed:

Highlights:

People who made it special:

What surprised me most:

Did it live up to my expectations?

1 2 3 4 5 6 7 8 9 10

## PLACE OR ADVENTURE:

**Target date:**

**Cost:**

**How to make it happen:**

**Planning details** (who with, where to stay, how to get there, what to bring):

Date completed: ..........

Highlights: ..........

People who made it special: ..........

What surprised me most: ..........

Did it live up to my expectations?

1 2 3 4 5 6 7 8 9 10

# PLACE OR ADVENTURE:

**Target date:**

**Cost:**

**How to make it happen:**

**Planning details** (who with, where to stay, how to get there, what to bring):

Date completed: ..........

Highlights: ..........

People who made it special: ..........

What surprised me most: ..........

Did it live up to my expectations?

1 2 3 4 5 6 7 8 9 10

## PLACE OR ADVENTURE:

**Target date:**

**Cost:**

**How to make it happen:**

**Planning details** (who with, where to stay, how to get there, what to bring):

Date completed:

Highlights:

People who made it special:

What surprised me most:

Did it live up to my expectations?

1 2 3 4 5 6 7 8 9 10

## PLACE OR ADVENTURE:

**Target date:**

**Cost:**

**How to make it happen:**

**Planning details** (who with, where to stay, how to get there, what to bring):

Date completed:

Highlights:

People who made it special:

What surprised me most:

Did it live up to my expectations?

1 2 3 4 5 6 7 8 9 10

## PLACE OR ADVENTURE:

Target date:

Cost:

How to make it happen:

**Planning details** (who with, where to stay, how to get there, what to bring):

Date completed:

Highlights:

People who made it special:

What surprised me most:

Did it live up to my expectations?

1 2 3 4 5 6 7 8 9 10

# PLACE OR ADVENTURE:

**Target date:**

**Cost:**

**How to make it happen:**

**Planning details** (who with, where to stay, how to get there, what to bring):

Date completed:

Highlights:

People who made it special:

What surprised me most:

Did it live up to my expectations?

1 2 3 4 5 6 7 8 9 10

# PLACE OR ADVENTURE:

Target date:

Cost:

How to make it happen:

**Planning details** (who with, where to stay, how to get there, what to bring):

Date completed: ............

Highlights: ............

People who made it special: ............

What surprised me most: ............

Did it live up to my expectations?

1 2 3 4 5 6 7 8 9 10

## PLACE OR ADVENTURE:

**Target date:**

**Cost:**

**How to make it happen:**

**Planning details** (who with, where to stay, how to get there, what to bring):

Date completed:

Highlights:

People who made it special:

What surprised me most:

Did it live up to my expectations?

1 2 3 4 5 6 7 8 9 10

## PLACE OR ADVENTURE:

Target date:

Cost:

How to make it happen:

**Planning details** (who with, where to stay, how to get there, what to bring):

Date completed:

Highlights:

People who made it special:

What surprised me most:

Did it live up to my expectations?

1 2 3 4 5 6 7 8 9 10

## PLACE OR ADVENTURE:

**Target date:**

**Cost:**

**How to make it happen:**

**Planning details** (who with, where to stay, how to get there, what to bring):

Date completed:

Highlights:

People who made it special:

What surprised me most:

Did it live up to my expectations?

1 2 3 4 5 6 7 8 9 10

## PLACE OR ADVENTURE:

**Target date:**

**Cost:**

**How to make it happen:**

**Planning details** (who with, where to stay, how to get there, what to bring):

Date completed:

Highlights:

People who made it special:

What surprised me most:

Did it live up to my expectations?

1 2 3 4 5 6 7 8 9 10

## PLACE OR ADVENTURE:

**Target date:**

**Cost:**

**How to make it happen:**

**Planning details** (who with, where to stay, how to get there, what to bring):

Date completed: ..........

Highlights: ..........

People who made it special: ..........

What surprised me most: ..........

Did it live up to my expectations?

1 2 3 4 5 6 7 8 9 10

# PLACE OR ADVENTURE:

**Target date:**

**Cost:**

**How to make it happen:**

**Planning details** (who with, where to stay, how to get there, what to bring):

Date completed:

Highlights:

People who made it special:

What surprised me most:

Did it live up to my expectations?

1 2 3 4 5 6 7 8 9 10

# PLACE OR ADVENTURE:

**Target date:**

**Cost:**

**How to make it happen:**

**Planning details** (who with, where to stay, how to get there, what to bring):

Date completed:

Highlights:

People who made it special:

What surprised me most:

Did it live up to my expectations?

1 2 3 4 5 6 7 8 9 10

# PLACE OR ADVENTURE:

Target date:

Cost:

How to make it happen:

**Planning details** (who with, where to stay, how to get there, what to bring):

Date completed:

Highlights:

People who made it special:

What surprised me most:

Did it live up to my expectations?

1 2 3 4 5 6 7 8 9 10

## PLACE OR ADVENTURE:

**Target date:**

**Cost:**

**How to make it happen:**

**Planning details** (who with, where to stay, how to get there, what to bring):

Date completed:

Highlights:

People who made it special:

What surprised me most:

Did it live up to my expectations?

1 2 3 4 5 6 7 8 9 10

## PLACE OR ADVENTURE:

**Target date:**

**Cost:**

**How to make it happen:**

**Planning details** (who with, where to stay, how to get there, what to bring):

Date completed:

Highlights:

People who made it special:

What surprised me most:

Did it live up to my expectations?

1 2 3 4 5 6 7 8 9 10

## PLACE OR ADVENTURE:

Target date:

Cost:

How to make it happen:

**Planning details** (who with, where to stay, how to get there, what to bring):

Date completed:

Highlights:

People who made it special:

What surprised me most:

Did it live up to my expectations?

1 2 3 4 5 6 7 8 9 10

## PLACE OR ADVENTURE:

Target date:

Cost:

How to make it happen:

**Planning details** (who with, where to stay, how to get there, what to bring):

Date completed: ...............................................................................

Highlights: ...............................................................................

...............................................................................

...............................................................................

...............................................................................

...............................................................................

...............................................................................

...............................................................................

...............................................................................

...............................................................................

People who made it special: ...............................................................................

...............................................................................

...............................................................................

...............................................................................

What surprised me most: ...............................................................................

...............................................................................

...............................................................................

...............................................................................

**Did it live up to my expectations?**

1 2 3 4 5 6 7 8 9 10

## PLACE OR ADVENTURE:

**Target date:**

**Cost:**

**How to make it happen:**

**Planning details** (who with, where to stay, how to get there, what to bring):

Date completed:

Highlights:

People who made it special:

What surprised me most:

Did it live up to my expectations?

1 2 3 4 5 6 7 8 9 10

## PLACE OR ADVENTURE:

**Target date:**

**Cost:**

**How to make it happen:**

**Planning details** (who with, where to stay, how to get there, what to bring):

Date completed:

Highlights:

People who made it special:

What surprised me most:

Did it live up to my expectations?

1 2 3 4 5 6 7 8 9 10

## PLACE OR ADVENTURE:

Target date:

Cost:

How to make it happen:

**Planning details** (who with, where to stay, how to get there, what to bring):

Date completed:

Highlights:

People who made it special:

What surprised me most:

Did it live up to my expectations?

1 2 3 4 5 6 7 8 9 10

# PLACE OR ADVENTURE:

Target date:

Cost:

How to make it happen:

**Planning details** (who with, where to stay, how to get there, what to bring):

Date completed:

Highlights:

People who made it special:

What surprised me most:

Did it live up to my expectations?

1 2 3 4 5 6 7 8 9 10

# PLACE OR ADVENTURE:

Target date:

Cost:

How to make it happen:

**Planning details** (who with, where to stay, how to get there, what to bring):

Date completed:

Highlights:

People who made it special:

What surprised me most:

Did it live up to my expectations?

1 2 3 4 5 6 7 8 9 10

## PLACE OR ADVENTURE:

Target date:

Cost:

How to make it happen:

**Planning details** (who with, where to stay, how to get there, what to bring):

Date completed:

Highlights:

People who made it special:

What surprised me most:

Did it live up to my expectations?

1 2 3 4 5 6 7 8 9 10

## PLACE OR ADVENTURE:

..........

..........

..........

..........

**Target date:** ..........

**Cost:** ..........

**How to make it happen:** ..........

..........

..........

..........

..........

**Planning details** (who with, where to stay, how to get there, what to bring):

..........

..........

..........

..........

..........

..........

..........

..........

Date completed:

Highlights:

People who made it special:

What surprised me most:

Did it live up to my expectations?

1 2 3 4 5 6 7 8 9 10

## PLACE OR ADVENTURE:

**Target date:**

**Cost:**

**How to make it happen:**

**Planning details** (who with, where to stay, how to get there, what to bring):

Date completed:

Highlights:

People who made it special:

What surprised me most:

Did it live up to my expectations?

1 2 3 4 5 6 7 8 9 10

# PLACE OR ADVENTURE:

Target date:

Cost:

How to make it happen:

**Planning details** (who with, where to stay, how to get there, what to bring):

Date completed: ..................

Highlights: ..................

People who made it special: ..................

What surprised me most: ..................

Did it live up to my expectations?

1 2 3 4 5 6 7 8 9 10

## PLACE OR ADVENTURE:

**Target date:**

**Cost:**

**How to make it happen:**

**Planning details** (who with, where to stay, how to get there, what to bring):

Date completed: ..........

Highlights: ..........

..........

..........

..........

..........

..........

..........

..........

..........

..........

People who made it special: ..........

..........

..........

..........

What surprised me most: ..........

..........

..........

..........

Did it live up to my expectations?

1 2 3 4 5 6 7 8 9 10

## PLACE OR ADVENTURE:

**Target date:**

**Cost:**

**How to make it happen:**

**Planning details** (who with, where to stay, how to get there, what to bring):

Date completed: ........................................

Highlights: ........................................

People who made it special: ........................................

What surprised me most: ........................................

Did it live up to my expectations?

1 2 3 4 5 6 7 8 9 10

# PLACE OR ADVENTURE:

Target date:

Cost:

How to make it happen:

**Planning details** (who with, where to stay, how to get there, what to bring):

Date completed: ..........

Highlights: ..........

..........

..........

..........

..........

..........

..........

..........

..........

..........

People who made it special: ..........

..........

..........

..........

What surprised me most: ..........

..........

..........

..........

Did it live up to my expectations?

1 2 3 4 5 6 7 8 9 10

## PLACE OR ADVENTURE:

**Target date:**

**Cost:**

**How to make it happen:**

**Planning details** (who with, where to stay, how to get there, what to bring):

Date completed: ........................................

Highlights: ........................................

........................................

........................................

........................................

........................................

........................................

........................................

........................................

........................................

........................................

People who made it special: ........................................

........................................

........................................

........................................

What surprised me most: ........................................

........................................

........................................

........................................

Did it live up to my expectations?

1 2 3 4 5 6 7 8 9 10

## PLACE OR ADVENTURE:

Target date:

Cost:

How to make it happen:

**Planning details** (who with, where to stay, how to get there, what to bring):

Date completed:

Highlights:

People who made it special:

What surprised me most:

Did it live up to my expectations?

1 2 3 4 5 6 7 8 9 10

## PLACE OR ADVENTURE:

Target date:

Cost:

How to make it happen:

**Planning details** (who with, where to stay, how to get there, what to bring):

Date completed:

Highlights:

People who made it special:

What surprised me most:

Did it live up to my expectations?

1 2 3 4 5 6 7 8 9 10

## PLACE OR ADVENTURE:

Target date:

Cost:

How to make it happen:

**Planning details** (who with, where to stay, how to get there, what to bring):

Date completed:

Highlights:

People who made it special:

What surprised me most:

Did it live up to my expectations?

1 2 3 4 5 6 7 8 9 10

# PLACE OR ADVENTURE:

**Target date:**

**Cost:**

**How to make it happen:**

**Planning details** (who with, where to stay, how to get there, what to bring):

Date completed:

Highlights:

People who made it special:

What surprised me most:

Did it live up to my expectations?

1 2 3 4 5 6 7 8 9 10

## PLACE OR ADVENTURE:

**Target date:**

**Cost:**

**How to make it happen:**

**Planning details** (who with, where to stay, how to get there, what to bring):

Date completed:

Highlights:

People who made it special:

What surprised me most:

Did it live up to my expectations?

1 2 3 4 5 6 7 8 9 10

## PLACE OR ADVENTURE:

..................................................

..................................................

..................................................

..................................................

**Target date:** ..................................................

**Cost:** ..................................................

**How to make it happen:** ..................................................

..................................................

..................................................

..................................................

..................................................

**Planning details** (who with, where to stay, how to get there, what to bring):

..................................................

..................................................

..................................................

..................................................

..................................................

..................................................

..................................................

..................................................

Date completed:

Highlights:

People who made it special:

What surprised me most:

Did it live up to my expectations?

1 2 3 4 5 6 7 8 9 10

*Books are a uniquely portable magic.*

STEPHEN KING

Your book bucket list might include childhood favorites to revisit (*Winnie-the-Pooh, The Hobbit, Charlotte's Web, The Golden Compass* . . . ), ambitious classics you never got around to reading (*The Canterbury Tales, Paradise Lost, Crime and Punishment, The Art of War*), and a few guilty pleasures that are just fun to read!

| BOOKS TO READ | PRIORITY RATING (1-10) | COMPLETED (DATE) |
|---|---|---|
| | | |
| | | |
| | | |
| | | |
| | | |
| | | |
| | | |
| | | |
| | | |
| | | |
| | | |
| | | |
| | | |
| | | |
| | | |
| | | |
| | | |
| | | |
| | | |

| BOOKS TO READ | PRIORITY RATING (1-10) | COMPLETED (DATE) |
|---|---|---|
| | | |
| | | |
| | | |
| | | |
| | | |
| | | |
| | | |
| | | |
| | | |
| | | |
| | | |
| | | |
| | | |
| | | |
| | | |
| | | |
| | | |
| | | |
| | | |

| BOOKS TO READ | PRIORITY RATING (1-10) | COMPLETED (DATE) |
|---|---|---|
| | | |
| | | |
| | | |
| | | |
| | | |
| | | |
| | | |
| | | |
| | | |
| | | |
| | | |
| | | |
| | | |
| | | |
| | | |
| | | |
| | | |
| | | |
| | | |

# MOVIES & SHOWS TO SEE

*All we have to decide is what to do with the time that is given to us.*

GANDALF, FROM *THE LORD OF THE RINGS: THE FELLOWSHIP OF THE RING*

This is probably the easiest category on your bucket list—it's easy to come up with ideas for movies and shows you'd love to see, and easy to make it happen. Whether you're watching *Butch Cassidy and the Sundance Kid* or the original *Star Wars* for the third time, or you're working your way through all the Best Picture Oscar movies, or seeking out *Hamilton* on Broadway, are you not entertained?

| MOVIES & SHOWS TO SEE | PRIORITY RATING (1-10) | DONE (DATE) |
| --- | --- | --- |
| | | |
| | | |
| | | |
| | | |
| | | |
| | | |
| | | |
| | | |
| | | |
| | | |
| | | |
| | | |
| | | |
| | | |
| | | |
| | | |
| | | |
| | | |
| | | |

| MOVIES & SHOWS TO SEE | PRIORITY RATING (1-10) | DONE (DATE) |
|---|---|---|
| | | |
| | | |
| | | |
| | | |
| | | |
| | | |
| | | |
| | | |
| | | |
| | | |
| | | |
| | | |
| | | |
| | | |
| | | |
| | | |
| | | |
| | | |
| | | |

| MOVIES & SHOWS TO SEE | PRIORITY RATING (1-10) | DONE (DATE) |
|---|---|---|
| | | |
| | | |
| | | |
| | | |
| | | |
| | | |
| | | |
| | | |
| | | |
| | | |
| | | |
| | | |
| | | |
| | | |
| | | |
| | | |
| | | |
| | | |

# FOODIE EXPERIENCES to RELISH

*Your body is not a temple, it's an amusement park. Enjoy the ride.*

ANTHONY BOURDAIN

This category could include notable restaurants or clubs to try, elaborate dishes to prepare, a special occasion bash to orchestrate, exotic cuisines or cocktails to sample, or whatever your appetite has dreamed of. Perhaps revisiting a childhood haunt, "Puttin' on the Ritz" at a 3-star restaurant, or taking a food trip filled with indulgences—from barbeque to bistros, from food trucks to mom-and-pop diners, and from local brews to mint juleps.

| GASTRONOMICAL WISH LIST | PRIORITY RATING (1-10) | DONE (DATE) |
| --- | --- | --- |
| | | |
| | | |
| | | |
| | | |
| | | |
| | | |
| | | |
| | | |
| | | |
| | | |
| | | |
| | | |
| | | |
| | | |
| | | |
| | | |
| | | |
| | | |
| | | |

| GASTRONOMICAL WISH LIST | PRIORITY RATING (1-10) | DONE (DATE) |
|---|---|---|
| | | |
| | | |
| | | |
| | | |
| | | |
| | | |
| | | |
| | | |
| | | |
| | | |
| | | |
| | | |
| | | |
| | | |
| | | |
| | | |
| | | |
| | | |
| | | |

| GASTRONOMICAL WISH LIST | PRIORITY RATING (1-10) | DONE (DATE) |
|---|---|---|
| | | |
| | | |
| | | |
| | | |
| | | |
| | | |
| | | |
| | | |
| | | |
| | | |
| | | |
| | | |
| | | |
| | | |
| | | |
| | | |
| | | |
| | | |
| | | |

*We can change the world and make it a better place. It is in our hands to make a difference.*

NELSON MANDELA

A Bucket List doesn't have to be solely hedonistic. The world needs all the help we can give it these days. You could focus on global issues, like climate, or local causes, like mentoring a child. Volunteers are needed for all types of nonprofits, so it should be easy to match your preferences and proclivities with causes. It's a win-win for you and your community when you help out by doing what you enjoy. Socialize shelter dogs and cats, serve up meals in a food pantry, help clean up local parks, be a literacy volunteer, bring music into after-school programs, or pay friendly visits to nursing home residents. Practice random acts of kindness, help out during emergencies, or give blood. So many ways to make a difference! To combine travel with service, search out the growing number of voluntourism or ecotourism opportunities.

| GOOD WORKS TO DO | PRIORITY RATING (1-10) | DONE (DATE) |
|---|---|---|
| | | |
| | | |
| | | |
| | | |
| | | |
| | | |
| | | |
| | | |
| | | |
| | | |
| | | |
| | | |
| | | |
| | | |
| | | |
| | | |
| | | |
| | | |
| | | |

| GOOD WORKS TO DO | PRIORITY RATING (1-10) | DONE (DATE) |
|---|---|---|
| | | |
| | | |
| | | |
| | | |
| | | |
| | | |
| | | |
| | | |
| | | |
| | | |
| | | |
| | | |
| | | |
| | | |
| | | |
| | | |
| | | |
| | | |
| | | |

| GOOD WORKS TO DO | PRIORITY RATING (1-10) | DONE (DATE) |
| --- | --- | --- |
| | | |
| | | |
| | | |
| | | |
| | | |
| | | |
| | | |
| | | |
| | | |
| | | |
| | | |
| | | |
| | | |
| | | |
| | | |
| | | |
| | | |
| | | |
| | | |

# THINGS TO LEARN & ACHIEVE

*Live as if you were to die tomorrow.*
*Learn as if you were to live forever.*

MAHATMA GANDHI

Light up your life with learning. You may have spent your early years learning via mandatory classes in school, but now you're free to learn what you love. Think about what you've always wanted to do . . . and then do it! Learn a new language, musical instrument, type of dance, sport, strategy game, or hobby. Memorize a poem, become a Master Gardener, learn public speaking, delve into music or art appreciation, take a sommelier course, hone woodworking or watercolor painting skills. Enrich your life as you achieve your ideal weight, get that degree you never quite finished, hike a famous trail, build a treehouse . . . the list goes on, and it's up to you to make that list. To stay engaged in learning, it may help to read, listen to podcasts, take classes, intern in a different field, or find a tribe of like minds by seeking out groups through Meetup or other social networks.

| THINGS TO LEARN & ACHIEVE | PRIORITY RATING (1-10) | DONE (DATE) |
|---|---|---|
| | | |
| | | |
| | | |
| | | |
| | | |
| | | |
| | | |
| | | |
| | | |
| | | |
| | | |
| | | |
| | | |
| | | |
| | | |
| | | |
| | | |
| | | |
| | | |

| THINGS TO LEARN & ACHIEVE | PRIORITY RATING (1-10) | DONE (DATE) |
|---|---|---|
| | | |
| | | |
| | | |
| | | |
| | | |
| | | |
| | | |
| | | |
| | | |
| | | |
| | | |
| | | |
| | | |
| | | |
| | | |
| | | |
| | | |
| | | |
| | | |